BEST-EVER HOMEMADE RAMEN

Secrets of a Japanese Ramen Chef

SHIGEKAZU TAKANASHI

TUTTLE Publishing

Tokyo | Rutland, Vermont | Singapore

CONTENTS

Why I Wrote This Book

Pleasure to meet you! My name is Shigekazu Takanashi, and I run a restaurant called Ramen Rotas in the town of Shimizu in Shizuoka Prefecture, Japan. My favorite food is ramen—of course! I think about ramen all day long, not only in terms of taste, but also in terms of the restaurant business and the working environment for the staff.

I have a goal. One day, I want everyone to eat the ramen I make.

Although I offer ramen kits through my online shop, most of my customers are local, so it's hard to reach people nationwide. That's why I started focusing on YouTube. Under the username ge-c, I uploaded daily videos of myself making ramen, and soon my channel had over 130,000 subscribers (it's more than double that now). People started writing to say they'd made my ramen at home after watching the videos.

I think ramen makes people happy.

When someone cooks one of my recipes for their family, I imagine them smiling as they sit around the table together enjoying it. I feel so lucky to be at the start of that chain of smiles.

As a way of showing my gratitude for everyone who has eaten my ramen or made it at home, I decided to compile my favorite recipes into a book. I put everything I've got into this book, and I promise that it will teach you the basics of making ramen. From that point on, you'll be able to pursue your own unique flavors. After all, there is no one right answer when it comes to ramen.

So let's get cooking and start spreading the smiles!

—Shigekazu Takanashi
Owner, Ramen Rotas

Your Ramen Kitchen

You can cook ramen successfully with fairly basic equipment, but the right tools make everything easier. These are the items I think are essential for making your best-ever homemade ramen.

1 Stockpot A large, deep pot is essential for making broth.

2 Cooking chopsticks Very useful for stirring, and better than a spoon for picking up ingredients.

3 Ladle Used for transferring broth and seasonings to the serving bowl.

4 Thermometer Carefully monitoring cooking temperature is a pro trick for better results.

5 Colander or sieve with handle Used to drain boiled noodles and strain broths.

6 Cooking pot For noodles. They taste better boiled in plenty of water, so make sure your pot is big enough. A lid is useful to have.

7 Tongs Mainly used to grab ingredients, but also handy for stirring and tossing.

8 Skillet For making flavored fat and stir-fries. It's convenient to have a few.

9 Turner Essential for cooking gyoza dumplings.

10 Wooden spatula For stir-frying.

11 Stainless steel pot Used for warming broth and simmering chashu pork. A small saucepan works best.

12 Digital scale Measuring ingredients correctly is the first step to making better ramen.
13 Whisk Key for thoroughly combining sauces and dips
14 Measuring cup Even a slight difference in quantities affects the flavor of broth and other recipes. A good measuring cup helps!
15 Pressure cooker Tenderizes tough ingredients such as pig's feet and chicken bones. Useful when making broth.
16 Large cast iron wok or skillet For making fried rice, stir-fries and more.
17 Frying strainer Used to remove deep-fried onions and garlic when making flavored fat.
18 Fine mesh strainer For straining broth after it has cooked in the stockpot.
19 Grater For garlic and ginger. Look for a Japanese oroshigane grater with fine teeth, which will produce smoother results than a Western-style grater.
20 Small cast iron skillet For warming small amounts of flavored fat and other ingredients.
21 Dashi stock bags These look like giant tea bags. Placing dried anchovies and bonito shavings in them when making broth saves the hassle of straining them out.
22 Mixing bowls Having several sizes is useful.
23 Rubber spatula Indispensable for scraping all the flavored fat or other sticky ingredients from a bowl or pan.
24 Serving bowl Serving your ramen in the right bowl makes it look tastier and hold its temperature better. Choose deep bowls that accommodate the amount of ramen you typically eat without too much extra room.

Your Ramen Pantry

Some ramens can be made with simple ingredients from a Western supermarket. But if you stock up on the items below at an Asian market or online shop, you'll be ready to make any recipe in this book. Choose higher quality ingredients whenever possible.

1 Dried anchovies (*niboshi*) A basic ingredient in dashi stock, the flavor of *niboshi* differs depending on size. I use mostly small *niboshi*, which have strong umami, with a few of the larger, more bitter variety as a flavor accent.

2 Bonito flakes (*katsuo-bushi*) These smoky, umami-rich shavings of fermented dried fish are worth seeking out. Thickly shaved flakes yield a robust oceany flavor in stock.

3 Kombu (dried kelp) Soak kombu in cold water overnight to make a richly flavored stock.

4 La-yu chili oil

5 Vegetable oil

6 Sesame oil

7 Lard

8 Butter

9 Dark soy sauce

10 Light soy sauce

11 Salt

12 Tamari soy sauce

13 White pepper

14 Sansho pepper

15 Red miso

16 White miso

17 Chinese-style stock paste

18 Oyster sauce

19 Scallop stock granules

20 Umami seasoning such as MSG

21 Rice vinegar

22 Mirin

23 Cooking sake

All About Noodles

For next-level ramen, match the type of ramen noodles to the type of broth you're using. This book uses store-bought noodles. The refrigerator or freezer section of an Asian market will have the most options.

1 Thin ramen noodles These silky noodles put the spotlight on the broth and go well with lighter soups.

2 Handmade ramen noodles Since they are made with more water than other varieties, handmade noodles have a softer texture. Perfect with a light shoyu broth.

3 Curly ramen noodles These versatile noodles match well with most broths. Thin wonton noodles work as a substitute.

4 Fettuccine These sturdy, wide noodles work surprisingly well in punchy soups and approximate certain regional ramen noodles. However, they are not made with kansui, the alkaline water that gives ramen noodles their distinctive chewiness.

5 Thick ramen noodles These hearty noodles play a leading role in dishes such as tsukemen (dipping noodles) and mazemen (mixed noodles). They're also used frequently in regional ramen dishes.

6 Dried ramen noodles These firm, robust noodles—which, unlike instant ramen noodles, are not deep-fried—can stand up to rich, assertive broths. They can be purchased in bulk online.

The Five Elements of Ramen

The foundation of ramen has three elements: broth, a seasoning mixture called tare (literally "sauce") and fat. Add noodles and toppings and your bowl is complete. The possible combinations are infinite.

Broth Broth determines the direction of the ramen and ties all the elements together. Using plenty of umami-rich ingredients like chicken, pork and seafood (or kombu and mushrooms for a vegetarian version) is key. Without a good broth, you can't make good ramen.

Fat It's no exaggeration to say that fat is what gives restaurant ramen its incredible smell and taste. Rendered pork or chicken fat, sometimes flavored with aromatics like garlic or chili, works its magic to make the broth taste even better.

Noodles In the past, noodles were the star of the show, but these days they're more like a supporting actor that brings out the best in the broth. The perfect pairing of noodles and broth is one of ramen's great pleasures.

Tare Pronounced "ta-ray," this sauce gives each chef's ramen its unique character. It delivers both the delicious explosion of flavor when you take your first bite and the aftertaste that lingers in your mouth when you're done.

Toppings The joy of homemade ramen is being able to customize the toppings. Dress your bowl up with classic items like chashu pork, boiled eggs and fermented bamboo shoots, or try regional specialties like seafood and veggies.

How to Use This Book

A Note About the Recipes in This Book

- On pages 14 through 37 you'll find recipes for all the basic elements used to make the ramens in this book, such as broths and tares.
- I recommend weighing or measuring ingredients carefully the first few times you make each recipe.
- Metric and imperial quantities are not exact equivalents. They have been adjusted for ease of measuring and shopping.
- 1 tablespoon = 15 ml, 1 teaspoon = 5 ml and 1 cup = 243 ml
- A "pinch" is about ⅕ teaspoon.
- Steps such as washing, peeling and removing the stems of ingredients have been omitted.
- If a specific heat level is not mentioned, use medium heat.
- I recommend nonstick skillets, especially for less experienced cooks.
- Use a mildly flavored vegetable oil for deep-frying.
- Quantities and cooking times may need to be adjusted depending on the size and quality of ingredients, the cooking equipment you are using, and other factors.

Chapter 1

Best-Ever Homemade Shoyu Ramen

"Shoyu" means soy sauce, and the ramen by that name is both simple and deeply flavored. The version in this chapter can be prepared from scratch in just one hour, including the broth, tare, flavored fat, chashu pork and marinated egg. The result is surprisingly close to the delicious ramen you'll find at a Japanese ramen restaurant.

Basic Mixed Broth

Great homemade ramen starts here. Simply combine the ingredients and simmer. This all-purpose broth is full of umami and works well with any kind of ramen.

Enough for 4 to 5 servings of ramen

3½ oz (100 g) dried anchovies (*niboshi*)
8½ cups (2 l) water
1 lb (500 g) pork belly
14 oz (400 g) ground chicken
1 large green onion or small leek, green part only
2 slices ginger
5-inch-square (½ oz/12 g) piece kombu
2 cups (25 g) bonito flakes (*katsuobushi*)

Best-Ever Shio Ramen, page 42

Onomichi Ramen, page 72

Staff Meal Curry, page 92

1 Stuff the dried anchovies into a dashi stock bag (see page 7). Place in a stock pot with the water, pork, chicken, green onion or leek, ginger and kombu. Bring to a boil over high heat, stirring to break up the ground chicken.

2 When the broth comes to a boil, reduce heat to low and simmer for 30 minutes, uncovered.

3 Remove the boiled pork. → Reserve to make Pork Belly Chashu (page 18).

4 Stuff the bonito shavings into another dashi stock bag. Add to the pot and simmer over low heat for 3 minutes.

5 Remove both stock bags and strain the broth through a fine mesh strainer into a bowl. → Use the ground chicken in Stir-Fried Greens with Ground Chicken (page 97). Use the anchovies in Crunchy Anchovy Chili Crisp (page 100).

Pro Tips

- Don't skim off the scum that rises to the top. It adds flavor and will be strained out at the end.
- To ensure a clear broth, don't cover the pot while simmering.
- Stuffing the dried anchovies into a dashi stock bags makes it easier to reuse them in the Crunchy Anchovy Chili Crisp. A cheesecloth pouch can be substituted.
- The broth keeps for 5 days in the refrigerator or a month in the freezer.

All-Purpose Shoyu Tare

This versatile sauce can be used to make chashu pork, marinated eggs, fried rice and more. But it's absolutely essential to making ramen! With this simple, deeply flavored version on hand, you can achieve restaurant-quality flavor in minutes.

About 4 cups

2½ cups (600 ml) dark soy sauce
1¼ cups (300 ml) water
5 tablespoons mirin
2 tablespoons cooking sake
1 tablespoon sugar
One large green onion or small leek, green part only
1 clove garlic
2 slices ginger

Takeoka Ramen, page 68

Tokushima Ramen, page 70

Green Onion and Chashu with Rice, page 90

1 Combine all ingredients in a medium saucepan over high heat, whisking to dissolve sugar.

2 When the tare comes to a boil, remove from heat and strain.

Pro Tips

- Use extra All-Purpose Shoyu Tare to make Marinated Jammy Eggs (page 20), Pork Belly Chashu (page 18), stir-fries or fried rice.
- Keeps for about 2 months in the refrigerator. Tare left over from making Pork Belly Chashu or Marinated Jammy Eggs keeps for 3 days in the refrigerator and can be reused.

Aromatic Fat

Richly flavored fat is a must-have for great ramen, so don't skip it! The savory flavor of green onions cooked in rendered fat sets this version apart. Chicken skin, pork lard, and fragrant seasonings add delicious layers of flavor.

Enough for 7 to 8 servings of ramen

3½ oz (100 g) pork lard
½ teaspoon sesame oil
5 oz (150 g) chicken skin
1 medium green onion, sliced
1 small garlic clove, quartered lengthwise
5 dried Japanese chili peppers, sliced

Pro Tips

- Keep the heat low so the green onion and chicken skins don't burn.
- Quarter the garlic lengthwise rather than thinly slicing to prevent burning.
- When the green onion and garlic are lightly browned, the fat is ready.

1 Warm the lard, sesame oil and chicken skin in a skillet over medium heat. When the fat begins to make spitting sounds, reduce heat to low and add the minced green onion, garlic and chili pepper.

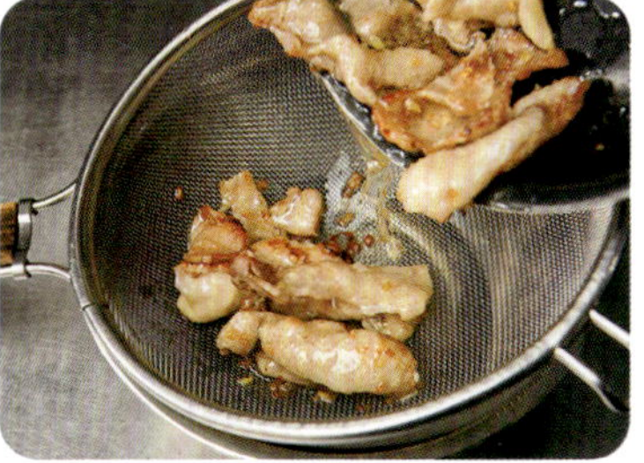

2 Cook for 10 minutes, stirring often. Pour through a fine mesh strainer. Save the bits of fried green onion, garlic and chili to add to ramen bowls. Use the chicken skins to make Chicken Cracklings with Ponzu (page 99).

Best-Ever Homemade Shoyu Ramen, page 22

Pork Belly Chashu

Recreating the thinly sliced pork that tops restaurant ramen is easy. Japanese chashu is an offshoot of Chinese char siu, but it's braised rather than roasted. This recipe uses pork left over from making Basic Mixed Broth, either marinated or simmered again in All-Purpose Shoyu Tare.

Enough for 4 to 5 servings of ramen

1 lb (500 g) cooked pork belly, reserved from making Basic Mixed Broth (page 14)

For the Twice-Simmered Chashu:
3 cups (800 ml) All-Purpose Shoyu Tare (page 16)

For the Marinated Chashu:
1¼ cups (300 ml) All-Purpose Shoyu Tare (page 16)

Sapporo Miso Ramen, page 40

Abura Soba, page 48

Ramen Restaurant Fried Rice, page 88

Green Onion and Chashu with Rice, page 90

Twice-Simmered Chashu

1 Put the tare and cooked pork belly in a pot that just fits the meat. Bring to a boil over medium heat.

2 Reduce heat to low and simmer for 10 minutes. Turn and cook on the other side for 10 minutes. Remove from sauce. The sauce can be refrigerated for up to 3 days and reused.

Marinated Chashu

1 Put the tare and the cooked pork belly in a ziplock bag and seal. Marinate for 6 hours in the refrigerator. Remove from sauce. The sauce can be refrigerated for up to 3 days and reused.

Pro Tips

- Choose a block of pork belly with plenty of fat. You can also use pork shoulder.
- If you are short on time, make the twice-simmered version. If you want to use less tare, make the marinated version.
- The chashu will keep, double-wrapped in cling film, for 5 days in the refrigerator and for about a month in the freezer.

Marinated Jammy Eggs

Super easy! Instead of garnishing your ramen with a plain boiled egg, try one of these for another layer of umami.

Makes 6 eggs

6 cups (1½ l) water
1 tablespoon vinegar
1 tablespoon salt
6 medium eggs
1 cup (200 ml) All-Purpose Shoyu Tare (page 16)

Best-Ever Shio Ramen, page 42

Abura Soba, page 48

Chilled Ramen, page 56

1 Combine the water, vinegar and salt in a saucepan over high heat.

2 Take the eggs out of the refrigerator and make a hole in the bottom of each one with a push pin or similar tool.

3 When the water comes to a boil, place the eggs in a strainer and lower them gently into the boiling water, taking care that they do not crack. Boil for 7 minutes over medium heat and an additional 1 minute over high heat.

4 Transfer the boiled eggs to ice water to cool.

5 When the eggs are cool, peel them and marinate in the tare for 40 minutes.

Pro Tips

- Salt raises the boiling point of water and vinegar coagulates proteins, so the eggs cook quickly.
- To prevent the eggs from hardening, make sure the marinade is cool before using.
- For even better results, marinate the eggs in ½ cup (100 ml) All-Purpose Shoyu Tare mixed with ½ cup (100 ml) water for at least 6 hours.
- The All-Purpose Shoyu Tare will keep for 3 days in the refrigerator after using, and can be reused 2 more times.

Best-Ever Homemade Shoyu Ramen

Once you have the elements made, this classic ramen is a snap to put together. Savory strips of fermented bamboo shoot called *menma* and slices of *naruto* fishcake with a pink swirl are traditional toppings, but the bowl is also tasty without them.

Serves 1

1 hank fresh curly ramen noodles, 4 to 5 oz (130 g)

For the soup:
3 tablespoons + 1 teaspoon All-Purpose Shoyu Tare (page 16)
1 tablespoon Aromatic Fat (page 17)
A pinch of fried green onion, garlic and chili bits reserved from making the Aromatic Fat
1¼ cups (300 ml) Basic Mixed Broth (page 14)

For the toppings:
2 slices Pork Belly Chashu (page 18)
1 Marinated Jammy Egg (page 20)
5 strips fermented bamboo shoot (*menma*), optional
1 tablespoon chopped green onion
1 slice *naruto* fish cake, optional
1 snack-size piece nori

1 Put the tare and fat in a serving bowl.

2 Add the fried green onion, garlic and chili bits to the bowl.

3 Cook the ramen noodles in plenty of boiling water following package instructions.

4 While the noodles cook, bring the broth to a simmer in a small saucepan and add to the bowl.

5 Thoroughly drain the noodles and add to the bowl. Garnish with the toppings and serve.

Pro Tips

- Scoop out the noodles with a one-handled strainer to avoid burning yourself. This also allows you to reuse the boiling water for another serving of ramen. Preparing ramen one serving at a time ensures the portions are right and it's piping hot.
- The fried green onion, garlic and chili add a great accent to the soup, but a little goes a long way.

Timetable

For Making Best-Ever Homemade Shoyu Ramen in One Hour

Making the main elements of this ramen—broth, tare, flavored fat, chashu pork and marinated egg—in just one hour might seem like a tall order. Actually, it's easy. All you need are two burners and a solid plan of action. Your best-ever bowl of homemade ramen is closer than you think!

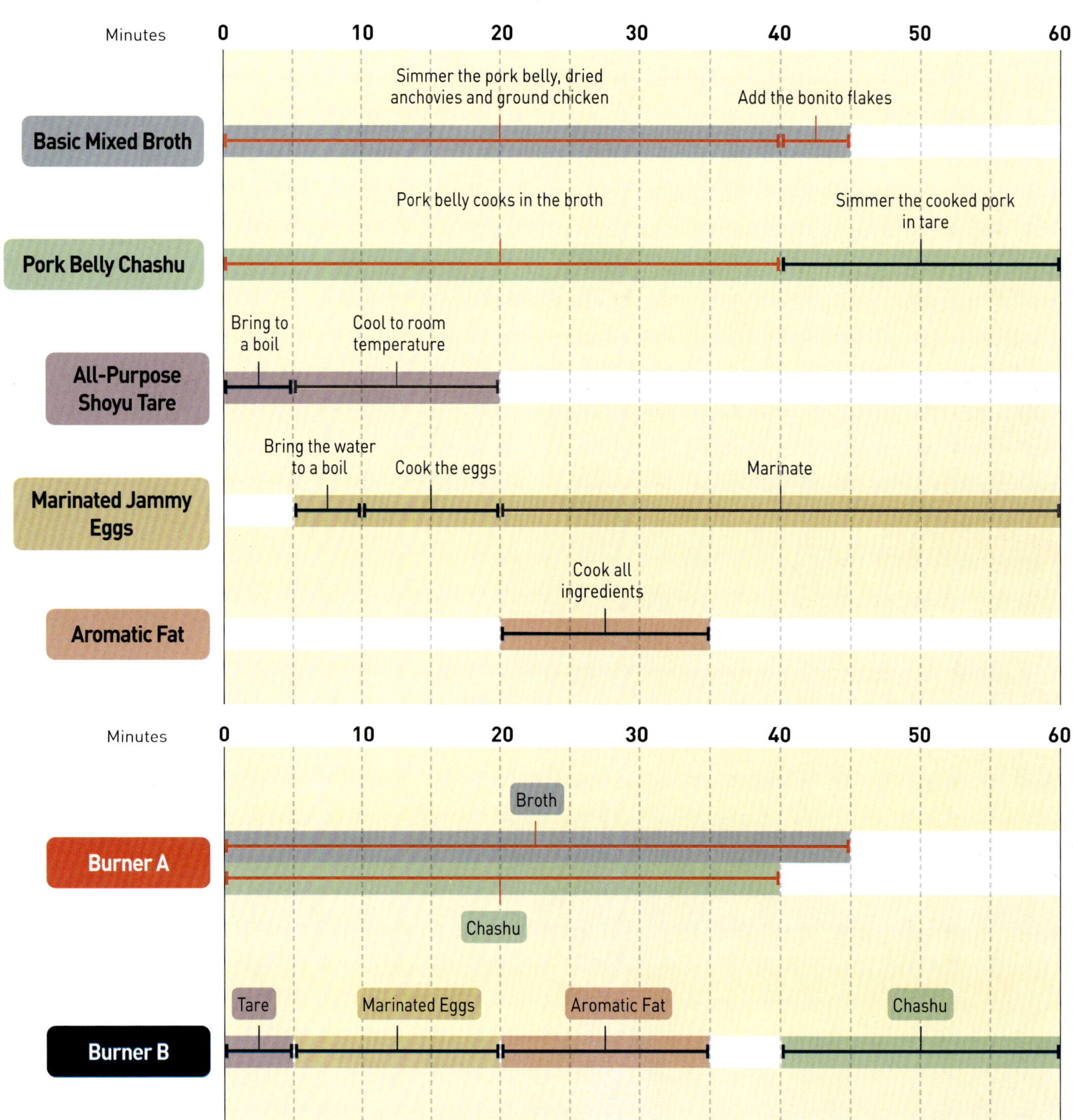

Chapter 2

Essential Recipes

Broth, tare and fat are the starting point for great homemade ramen. This chapter gives you variations on each element, from miso and shio (salt) tares to anchovy broth, and even a quick chicken chashu. By combining these elements in different ways, you can make a wide range of ramens in very little time.

Miso Tare

A richly flavored tare that blends two types of miso. By layering several strongly flavored ingredients, you'll create a powerful hit of umami that can stand up to any broth.

Enough for 4 to 5 servings of ramen

1/3 cup (100 g) white miso
1/3 cup (100 g) red miso
1 tablespoon sesame oil
1 tablespoon plus 1 teaspoon butter
4 cloves garlic, minced
4-inch (10 cm) piece ginger, minced
2 oz (50 g) ground pork
1 tablespoon + 1 teaspoon dark soy sauce
1 tablespoon mirin
1 tablespoon cooking sake
1 1/2 teaspoons umami seasoning, such as MSG
1 teaspoon oyster sauce
2 teaspoons scallop stock granules
1 tablespoon toasted sesame seeds

Sapporo Miso Ramen, page 40

1 Combine the white miso, red miso and sesame oil in a small bowl and mix well.

2 Heat a skillet over low heat, add the butter and minced garlic and ginger, and stir fry until fragrant. Be careful not to let the garlic and ginger burn.

3 Add the ground pork and stir-fry over medium heat.

4 When the meat changes color, add the dark soy sauce, mirin, cooking sake, umami seasoning, oyster sauce and stock granules to the skillet and continue stir-frying.

5 Add the stir-fried ingredients and the sesame seeds to the miso mixture. Mix well.

Pro Tips

- This tare has just the right blend of mellow white miso and pungent red miso.
- Stir-fried ground pork adds richness to the tare.

Shio Tare

This tare pleases the pickiest of palates without ever getting boring. Umami seasoning and scallop stock granules give it impact, while soy sauce adds the depth needed to balance any broth.

Enough for 4 to 5 servings of ramen

1½ cups (350 ml) water
3 tablespoons + 1 teaspoon cooking sake
2 tablespoons dark soy sauce
1 tablespoon + 1 teaspoon mirin
3 tablespoons salt
2 teaspoons umami seasoning, such as MSG
1 teaspoon scallop stock granules
1 small piece thickly shaved bonito (*atsukezuri katsuobushi*), about ¼ oz (7g), or ½ cup (7 g) thin bonito flakes

1 Combine the water, sake, dark soy sauce, mirin, salt, umami seasoning and stock granules in a small pot over high heat and stir to dissolve seasonings.

2 When the mixture comes to a boil, add the shaved bonito. Reduce heat to low and simmer for 10 minutes. Pour through a fine mesh strainer.

Best-Ever Shio Ramen, page 42
Nagasaki Chanpon Ramen, page 74

Pro Tips

- Raw cane sugar adds a mellower sweetness than refined white sugar.

Favorite Shoyu Tare

Outstanding flavor guaranteed. The secret to this sauce is its simplicity. Whenever I eat it, I remember that the point of shoyu ramen is to savor the deliciousness of soy sauce.

Enough for 4 to 5 servings of ramen

For the dark version:

⅔ cup (150 ml) dark soy sauce
1 tablespoon + 1 teaspoon tamari soy sauce
1 teaspoon mirin
1 scant teaspoon raw cane sugar or white sugar

For the light version:

⅔ cup (150 ml) light soy sauce
2 teaspoons mirin
2 teaspoons raw cane sugar or white sugar
1 teaspoon umami seasoning, such as MSG

1 For both the dark and light versions, combine all the ingredients in a small pot over high heat and stir to dissolve sugar.

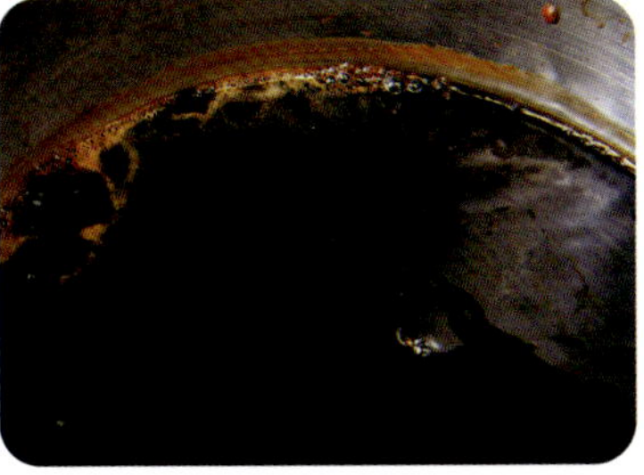

2 Remove from heat just before the mixture comes to a boil.

Ramen in Kombu Water, page 50

Iekei Ramen, page 52

Dried Anchovy Broth

Bursting with the flavor of the ocean. The goal here is a broth that fills your mouth with the distinctive taste of dried anchovies (*niboshi*). Large and small anchovies differ in flavor. Here they are combined for just the right balance.

Enough for 4 to 5 servings of ramen

10½ cups (2½ l) water
9 oz (250 g) small dried anchovies (*niboshi*)
5 oz (150 g) large dried anchovies (*niboshi*)
3-inch-square (1/5 oz/5 g) piece kombu
1 medium piece thickly shaved bonito (*atsukezuri katsuobushi*), about 1/3 oz (10 g), or 2/3 cup (10 g) thin bonito flakes
1 green onion, green part only
1 clove garlic

Dried Anchovy Ramen, page 46

Tsubame Sanjo Ramen, page 80

1 Combine all the ingredients in a stock pot.

2 Place over very low heat.

3 Cook for 40 minutes. Remove from heat when the liquid comes to boil, or if using a thermometer, when the temperature reaches 198°F (92°C).

4 Pour through a fine mesh strainer into a bowl.

Pro Tips

- *Niboshi* are a standard ingredient in dashi stock. Look for them at Asian markets.
- Small *niboshi* contribute a delicate umami, while large *niboshi* add a touch of bitterness along with their characteristic anchovy flavor.

Super Simple Chicken Broth

Ground meat and water make magic. Don't underestimate this extremely simple recipe. It produces a straightforward, delicious broth that works for most ramens. Use ground dark meat if you can find it; most supermarket ground chicken is a mix of white and dark meat, which is also fine.

Enough for 3 servings of ramen

14 oz (400 g) ground chicken
5 cups (1.2 l) water

Triple Chicken Shoyu Ramen, page 44

Ramen in Kombu Water, page 50

Chilled Ramen, page 56

1 Combine the water and ground chicken in a pot over medium heat, breaking up the meat with a spatula.

2 When the liquid comes to a boil, reduce heat to low and simmer for 20 minutes.

3 Pour through a fine mesh strainer into a bowl.

4 Use the leftover ground meat to make Stir-Fried Greens with Ground Chicken (page 97).

Pro Tips

- Don't skim the broth as it cooks. The scum provides a strong, gamey flavor that works great with ramen.
- Breaking up the ground chicken thoroughly allows more of its flavor to seep into the soup.

Chicken and Pork Paitan Broth

A rich, creamy broth. "Paitan" means "white soup." The ingredients are simmered slowly to extract all their flavor, yielding a cloudy white broth.

Serves 4 to 5

1 pork knuckle
1 pig's foot
3 chicken carcasses
Water as needed
1 clove garlic
1 large green onion or small leek, green part only

Sapporo Miso Ramen, page 40
Iekei Ramen, page 52
Dipping Noodles, page 54
Tokushima Ramen, page 70
Nagasaki Chanpon Ramen, page 74
Kyoto Ramen, page 82

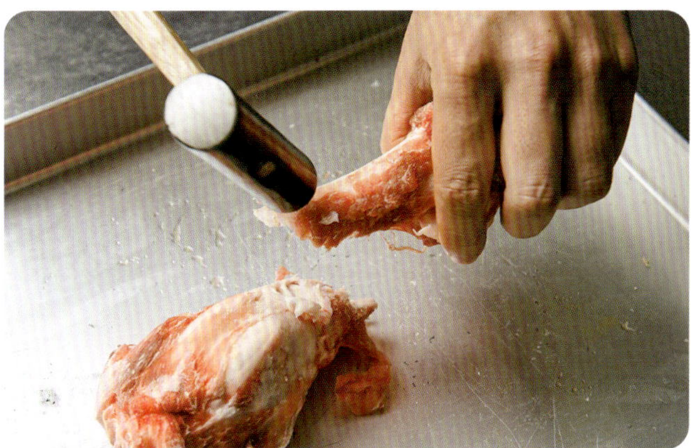

1 Bring a large pot of water to a boil. Bash the pork knuckle and chicken carcasses with a hammer and add to the boiling water.

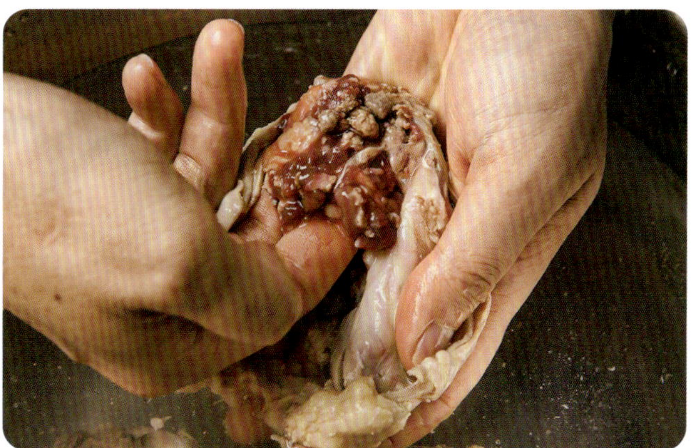

2 As soon as the water returns to a boil, remove the chicken carcasses and wash well under running water to remove any blood or organs. Boil the pork knuckle for an additional 5 minutes, then remove. Discard cooking water.

3 Place the parboiled pork knuckle and chicken carcasses in a large pressure cooker together with the pig's foot. Fill to maximum capacity with water, bring to pressure, and cook for 30 minutes.

4 Allow the pressure cooker to naturally depressurize. Open the lid, add 4 cups (1 liter) of water, and cook for 40 minutes to an hour over high heat, until the broth is as strong as you like, stirring occasionally.

5 Pour through a fine mesh strainer into a bowl.

Pro Tips

- Parboiling the chicken carcasses for too long results in lost flavor, so make sure to remove them quickly in step 2.
- If you can't pound the pork knuckle hard enough to crack it, ask the butcher to cut it in half.
- Stirring the soup often with a wooden spatula after you remove the pressure cooker lid will promote emulsification and make the soup thicker.
- Cooking down the soup for 40 minutes yields a lighter broth, and cooking for a full hour yields a richer one.

Pro Tips

- Green onion cuts the gamey odor of the chicken fat.
- To prevent the onion and green onion from burning, lower the heat as soon as they brown and remove them with a strainer or slotted spoon. Reserve to add to ramen bowls as a flavor accent.

Chicken Fat, Anchovy-Flavored Fat, and Double Onion Fat

These versatile flavored fats are useful for more than just ramen. Try them in fried rice and stir-fries, too. In ramen, they are a key flavor element and help the broth stick to the noodles.

For the Chicken Fat:
10 oz (300 g) chicken skin
One large green onion, green part only

For the Double Onion Fat:
¾ cup (150 g) lard
5 tablespoons minced onion
3 tablespoons minced green onion

For the Anchovy-Flavored Fat:
½ cup (100 g) lard
5 large dried anchovies (*niboshi*)

Sapporo Miso Ramen, page 40

Best-Ever Shio Ramen, page 42

Chicken Fat

1 Slice the green onion ¼ inch (5 mm) thick. Place the chicken skin and green onion in a skillet over medium heat.
2 When the chicken skin begins to release its fat, reduce the heat to low and cook for 5 minutes. Pour through a fine mesh strainer. Reserve the skin to make Chicken Cracklings (page 99).

Anchovy-Flavored Fat

1 Warm the lard in a skillet over low heat. When the lard has melted, add the dried anchovies.
2 Cook over very low heat for about 10 minutes. When the fat has taken on the aroma of the anchovies, pour through a fine mesh strainer.

Double Onion Fat

1 Put the lard in a skillet over high heat. When the lard has melted, add the onion and green onion and stir-fry.
2 When the onion and green onion start to color, reduce heat to low, stirring constantly so the onions do not burn. When they are fully browned, pour the fat through a fine mesh strainer.

Pro Tips

- The chicken will keep for 5 days, well wrapped in cling film, in the refrigerator.

Lazy Chicken Chashu

A simple and healthy alternative to pork chashu. This lightly flavored chicken is done in less than half an hour and goes well with any broth.

Enough for 4 to 5 servings of ramen

2 cups (450 ml) water
5 teaspoons salt
10 shakes or grinds of black pepper
2 boneless chicken breasts, about 1 lb (500 g) total

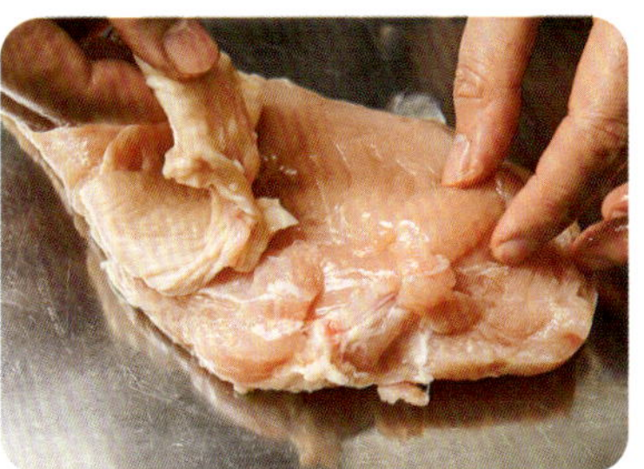

1 Bring the water, salt and black pepper to a boil in a medium pot. Remove the skin and any visible fat from the chicken breasts.

2 Add the chicken breasts to the boiling water. When the water returns to a boil, reduce the heat to low and cook for 20 minutes. Drain.

Best-Ever Shio Ramen, page 42

Fresh Spring Rolls with Chicken Chashu, page 98

I Owe It All to My Mentor

One morning, after I had stopped going to university and started spending my days sleeping, I woke up feeling like I was emerging from hibernation. I happened to pick up a recruitment magazine and spotted an ad for a job at a ramen restaurant. That's how it all started.

I got a job at the restaurant and learned the basics of business, such as cost of sales ratios and labor costs. I realized that a restaurant is a team, and that the restaurant will grow if everyone works together. I was fascinated by ramen as a business.

Five years later, I knocked on the door of a local ramen restaurant called Menya Nakagawa in Shimizu-cho, my home town, wanting to learn the fundamentals of ramen as a food. The restaurant was known for its shoyu ramen with seafood broth and its abura ramen, a soupless noodle dish. Around this time I started to dream of opening my own restaurant one day.

I'm a slow learner, but the boss helped me learn the ropes, and three years later, when I was 27, I decided it was time to start my own place. I had already chosen a property and paid a deposit, but suddenly I got nervous and gave up. I cried to the boss and he rehired me, and for the next three years I worked with a new resolve. I knew that if I didn't change, nothing would change. I thought about what it means to have your own restaurant, and I decided to learn everything I could from the example of my boss.

Three years later, he sent me off again, saying with a smile, "I'm sure you'll do fine." Two years after that my old boss—my mentor—walked into my restaurant, ordered a bowl, and praised my ramen. That may have been the day I gained confidence in the ramen I was making.

Chapter 3

Special Occasion Homemade Ramen

Once you've mastered the basics of ramen, why not challenge yourself to creating a bowl that's just a little bit better, from the seasonings to the toppings to the broth? In this chapter you'll find ten easy ramen recipes that can easily be the star of a special meal.

Sapporo Miso Ramen

A hearty winter ramen from Japan's snow country. Sapporo is the capital of Japan's northernmost island, Hokkaido. This is my take on the city's signature ramen, full of rich broth, flavorful miso and satisfying toppings.

Serves 1

1 hank fresh curly ramen noodles, 4 to 5 oz (130 g)

For the soup:

1¼ cups (300 ml) Chicken and Pork Paitan Broth (page 34)
⅓ cup (80 g) Miso Tare (page 26)
1 tablespoon Double Onion Fat (page 36)
Japanese ground chili pepper (*ichimi togarashi*), to taste

For the toppings:

3 slices Pork Belly Chashu (page 18)
½ cup (80 g) bean sprouts
5 strips fermented bamboo shoot (*menma*)
1½ tablespoons chopped green onion

1 Spoon the tare into a serving bowl and microwave for 30 seconds, until warm.
2 Heat the broth in a small saucepan and pour into the bowl. Whisk to dissolve the miso.
3 Cook the noodles in plenty of boiling water following package instructions. Place the bean sprouts in a handled strainer or basket. One minute before the noodles are done, lower the bean sprouts into the boiling water.
4 Remove the bean sprouts. Drain the noodles and add to the bowl. Garnish with the toppings.
5 Heat the Double Onion Fat in a small skillet and drizzle over the broth and toppings. Sprinkle with ground chili pepper.

Pro Tips

- To recreate the deep flavor of authentic Sapporo ramen, heat the Double Onion Fat to the smoke point.
- Miso Tare also works great with Basic Mixed Broth (page 14), Dried Anchovy Broth (page 30), and Iejiro Broth (page 60).

Best-Ever Shio Ramen

Simplicity is everything here. To showcase the flavor of the broth, the seasonings and toppings are kept light and uncomplicated.

Serves 1

1 hank fresh curly ramen noodles, 4 to 5 oz (130 g)

For the soup:

1¼ cups (300 ml) Basic Mixed Broth (page 14)
1 tablespoon + 2 teaspoons Shio Tare (page 28)
1 tablespoon Chicken Fat (page 36)

For the toppings:

2 slices Lazy Chicken Chashu (page 37)
½ Marinated Jammy Egg (page 20)
1 green onion, white part only
5 strips fermented bamboo shoot (*menma*)
1 teaspoon fried onions from making Double Onion Fat (page 36), optional

1 Place the tare and fat in a serving bowl. Warm the broth in a small saucepan and add to the bowl.
2 Cook the noodles in plenty of boiling water following package directions.
3 Finely chop the green onion in a food processor or by hand.
4 Drain the noodles and add to the bowl.
5 Garnish with the toppings.

Pro Tips

- Chopping the green onion in a food processor pulverizes them slightly, so their flavor dissolves into the broth better.
- Fried onions reserved from making the Double Onion Fat are a nice but non-essential accent.

Triple Chicken Shoyu Ramen

This ramen features three kinds of chicken: chicken broth, chicken fat added for flavor, and sliced chicken on top. The simple, elegant shoyu tare gives the dish a refined character.

Serves 1

1 hank fresh curly ramen noodles, 4 to 5 oz (130 g)

For the soup:

1¼ cups (300 ml) Super Simple Chicken Broth (page 32)
2 tablespoons + 1 teaspoon Favorite Shoyu Tare (dark version) (page 29)
1 tablespoon Chicken Fat (page 36)

For the toppings:

3 slices Lazy Chicken Chashu (page 37)
A few mitsuba or celery leaves
5 strips fermented bamboo shoot (*menma*)

1 Place the tare and 2 teaspoons of the fat in a serving bowl.
2 Warm the broth in a small saucepan and add to the bowl.
3 Cook the noodles in plenty of boiling water following package directions. Drain and add to the bowl.
4 Garnish with the toppings and the remaining teaspoon of fat.

Pro Tips

- Adding the chicken fat in two parts makes a big difference in the final results.
- Mitsuba is a delicately flavored Japanese herb available at some Japanese markets. Mild celery leaves can be substituted, although the flavor is quite different.

Dried Anchovy Ramen

Dried anchovies and soy sauce are a superb flavor duo. In this ramen, anchovies feature in both the broth and the flavored fat, while soy sauce stars in the tare.

Serves 1

1 hank fresh curly ramen noodles, 4 to 5 oz (130 g)

For the soup:
1¼ cups (300 ml) Dried Anchovy Broth (page 30)
1 tablespoon + 1 teaspoon Favorite Shoyu Tare (light version) (page 29)
2 teaspoons Anchovy-Flavored Fat (page 36)

For the toppings:
2 slices Pork Belly Chashu (page 18)
1 tablespoon thinly sliced green onion
5 strips fermented bamboo shoot (*menma*)
1 snack-sized sheet nori

1 Place the tare and fat in a serving bowl.
2 Warm the broth in a small saucepan and add to the bowl.
3 Cook the noodles in plenty of boiling water following package directions. Drain the noodles and add to the bowl.
4 Sear the chashu quickly in a hot pan, or by holding with tongs over a gas burner.
5 Garnish the ramen with the toppings.

Pro Tips

- To put more emphasis on the broth, substitute a mild vegetable oil for the Anchovy-Flavored Fat.
- Use the dark version of Favorite Shoyu Tare for an interesting variation.

Abura Soba

Also called mazemen or mazesoba, abura soba is ramen without the broth. My version is savory, hearty, and absolutely addictive.

Serves 1

1 hank fresh thick ramen noodles, 4 to 5 oz (130 g)

For the seasonings:
2 teaspoons dark soy sauce
1 tablespoon oyster sauce
1 teaspoon sweet yakiniku sauce
1 teaspoon sesame oil
2 teaspoons lard
A pinch of white pepper
⅓ teaspoon Chinese-style stock paste

For the toppings:
2 slices Pork Belly Chashu (page 18)
3 green onions, white part only
5 strips fermented bamboo shoot (*menma*)
Japanese ground chili pepper (*ichimi togarashi*) to taste
½ Marinated Jammy Egg (page 20)
Finely grated garlic to taste

1 Cut the green onion in half lengthwise and slice thinly on the diagonal. Rinse under running water.
2 Place the soy sauce, oyster sauce, yakiniku sauce, sesame oil, lard, white pepper and stock paste in a serving bowl and microwave for 30 seconds, until the lard melts. Mix well.
3 Cook the noodles in plenty of boiling water following package directions. Drain, add to the bowl and mix very well.
4 Garnish with the toppings.

Pro Tips

- I recommend thick noodles for this dish.
- Finely grating the garlic on a Japanese oroshigane or Western grater allows it to meld into the sauce better than chopping it would.
- Rinsing the green onions makes them milder and crunchier.

Ramen in Kombu Water

Kombu at its tastiest! Soaking this umami-rich kelp overnight in cold water with dried anchovies yields an amazingly tasty broth. As an added bonus, the kombu water has a viscous texture that clings well to the noodles. Dishes like this one, with a dipping sauce rather than a soup, typically are served with more noodles.

Serves 1

2 hanks fresh thick ramen noodles, about 10 oz (300 g)

For the kombu water (enough for 2 servings):

2¾ cups (650 ml) water
⅔ oz (20 g) dried anchovies (*niboshi*)
5 x 10 inch (1 oz/30 g) piece kombu

For the dipping sauce:

1 tablespoon + 2 teaspoons Favorite Shoyu Tare (dark version) (page 29)
2 teaspoons Chicken Fat (page 36)
½ cup (120 ml) Super Simple Chicken Broth (page 32)

For the toppings:

1 tablespoon thinly sliced green onion
5 strips fermented bamboo shoot (*menma*)
Several mitsuba or celery leaves
2 slices Pork Belly Chashu (page 18)
A pinch of salt
⅛ lemon

1 Put the water, dried anchovies and kombu in a quart jar and refrigerate overnight. Strain through a fine mesh strainer.

2 Cook the noodles in plenty of boiling water for twice as long as indicated on the package.

3 While the noodles cook, combine the tare, fat, and broth in a serving bowl.

4 Rinse the cooked noodles well under cold water and drain.

5 Place ¾ cup (180 ml) kombu water in another serving bowl and add the noodles. Serve the toppings and dipping sauce on the side. Squeeze the lemon into the sauce to taste.

Pro Tips

- If you really want to savor the umami of the kombu water, skip the dipping sauce and slurp with just a dash of salt.
- After you finish eating the noodles, you can add the remaining kombu water to the dipping sauce to make a tasty soup.

Iekei Ramen

A nostalgic ramen loaded with fresh veggies. Iekei is a type of ramen with hearty chicken and pork broth that originated in Yokohama but today is popular all over Japan. My version features an extra dose of green vegetables.

Serves 1

1 hank fresh, very thick ramen noodles, 4 to 5 oz (130 g)

For the soup:

2 tablespoons + 2 teaspoons Favorite Shoyu Tare (dark version) (page 29)
1 tablespoon + 1 teaspoon Chicken Fat (page 36)
1¼ cups (300 ml) Chicken and Pork Paitan Broth (page 34)
A pinch of umami seasoning, such as MSG

For the toppings:

½ cup (20 g) spinach
1 cabbage leaf
2 tablespoons thinly sliced green onions
3 snack-size sheets nori
2 slices Pork Belly Chashu (page 18)

1 Blanch the spinach for about 10 seconds, drain well and cut into 2-inch (5-cm) pieces. Roughly chop the cabbage.
2 Put the tare and fat in a serving bowl. Warm the broth in a small saucepan and add to the bowl along with the umami seasoning.
3 Cook the noodles in plenty of boiling water following package directions. Drain and add to the ramen bowl.
4 Garnish with the toppings.

Pro Tips

- Finely grated garlic is a tasty addition to the soup.
- Adjust the amount of tare and fat to taste, as well as the firmness of the boiled noodles.

Dipping Noodles

The thick, rich dipping sauce blends the flavors of pork, chicken and seafood. *Gyofun*, a powder made from various types of dried fish, is an essential ingredient here and well worth seeking out at an Asian market or online. It gives this dish the unmistakable fishy umami of a great ramen shop.

Serves 1

2 hanks fresh thick ramen noodles, about 10 oz (300 g)

For the dipping sauce:

2 tablespoons + 2 teaspoons Favorite Shoyu Tare (dark version) (page 29)
⅔ cup (150 ml) Chicken and Pork Paitan Broth (page 34)
1 tablespoon + 1 teaspoon Double Onion Fat (page 36)
1 teaspoon sugar
A pinch of umami seasoning, such as MSG
⅓ teaspoon Chinese stock paste
Japanese ground chili pepper (*ichimi togarashi*) to taste

For the toppings:

1 slice *naruto* fish cake
2 tablespoons thinly sliced green onion
1 snack-size sheet nori
5 strips fermented bamboo shoot (*menma*)
1 slice Pork Belly Chashu (page 18)
3 tablespoons *gyofun* fish powder

1 Combine the dipping sauce ingredients in a medium serving bowl and mix.
2 Microwave for 50 seconds and mix well again.
3 Cook the noodles in plenty of boiling water following package directions. Drain and rinse well under cold running water. Drain again and place in a large serving bowl.
4 Arrange the toppings in the dipping sauce bowl. Spoon the fish powder on top of the nori so that it doesn't dissolve right away.

Pro Tips

- The dipping sauce is best piping hot. If it cools too much while you're eating, just pop it back in the microwave to warm it up.
- When you make the Chicken and Pork Paitan Broth, I recommend boiling it down for a full hour to thicken and concentrate the flavors.

Chilled Ramen

Chilled ramen noodles topped with raw vegetables and chicken or ham is a favorite summer dish in Japan, called *hiyashi chuka*. Apple cider vinegar is the secret to my version, which tastes just as great any time of the year!

Serves 1

1 hank fresh thick ramen noodles, 4 to 5 oz (130 g)

For the toppings:
½ Marinated Jammy Egg (page 20)
2 slices Lazy Chicken Chashu (page 37)
5 green shiso leaves, shredded (optional)
Chinese Style Pickles, to taste (page 101)
Cherry tomatoes, to taste

For the sauce (makes about 2½ cups, enough for 5 servings):
⅔ cup (150 ml) dark soy sauce
⅔ cup minus 2 teaspoons (140 ml) apple cider vinegar
1 cup (240 ml) Basic Mixed Broth (page 14), Dried Anchovy Broth (page 30) or Super Simple Chicken Broth (page 32)
4 tablespoons sugar
2 tablespoons plus 1 teaspoon sesame oil
2 teaspoons umami seasoning, such as MSG

1 Combine the sauce ingredients in a storage container with a tight-fitting lid. Mix well and refrigerate.

2 Cook the noodles in plenty of boiling water for twice the amount of time indicated on the package. Drain and rinse well under cold running water, until the surface no longer feels sticky. Shake off excess water.

3 Pour ½ cup (100 ml) of the sauce into a serving bowl. Add the noodles and garnish with the toppings.

Pro Tips

- Apple cider vinegar is milder than grain vinegars and works especially well here.
- To substitute rice vinegar, bring to a boil in a small pot or microwave before adding to the sauce so it is less sharp.
- The sauce will keep in the refrigerator for 5 days.

Fastest-Ever Homemade Shoyu Ramen

So easy, so surprisingly good. Just add hot water to store-bought seasonings and you've got ramen not so different from what you'd get at a street-side stall in Japan.

Serves 1

1 hank fresh curly ramen noodles, 4 to 5 oz (130 g)

For the soup:
2 tablespoons dark soy sauce
1 teaspoon chicken stock granules
½ teaspoon scallop stock granules
½ teaspoon dashi stock granules
1 teaspoon lard
⅓ teaspoon Chinese soup stock paste
1¼ cups (300 ml) water

For the toppings:
2 slices chashu, store-bought
½ store-bought marinated egg or regular boiled egg
5 strips fermented bamboo shoot (*menma*)
1 tablespoon sliced green onion

1 Combine the dark soy sauce, chicken stock granules, scallop stock granules and dashi stock granules in a serving bowl. Bring the 1¼ cups water to a boil and add to the bowl.
2 Add the lard and stock paste to the bowl and stir to dissolve.
3 Cook the noodles in plenty of boiling water following package directions. Drain and add to the bowl.
4 Garnish with the toppings.

Pro Tips

- The various stock granules and paste can be bought at an Asian market. For the chicken stock granules, look for a variety without Western herbs.
- Chashu and marinated eggs (*ajitsuke tamago* or *ajitama*) are sold in the refrigerator section of Japanese and Asian markets.

Chapter 4

Infinite Impact Iejiro Ramen

If you want to understand the history of ramen in Japan, you have to understand Ramen Jiro, a chain of restaurants that originated in Tokyo in the 1960s selling huge, bold, cheap bowls of ramen. "Iejiro Ramen" is what Jiro fans call their attempts to replicate the deliciousness at home. The recipes in this chapter are my homage to Ramen Jiro's one-of-a-kind, over-the-top ramen.

Iejiro Broth, Iejiro Pork Back Fat and Iejiro Chashu

This amazingly rich, cloudy soup is done in just one hour. Make sure not to skim it as it boils, since the scum contains much of the flavor. The pork back fat, another key ingredient in Iejiro ramen, is prepared together with the broth, along with the chashu.

Serves 4 to 5

2½ quarts (2½ l) water
1 lb (500 g) pork belly
2 pig's feet
3 chicken drumettes
14 oz (400 g) pork back fat (fatback)
1 large green onion or leek, green part only
1 head garlic
All-Purpose Shoyu Tare (page 16), as needed

Iejiro Ramen, page 63

*Refer to the photo on page 62 to see how the pork back fat looks when done.

1 Slice the whole garlic head in half horizontally. Combine all the ingredients in a stockpot, cover and bring to a boil over high heat. Reduce heat to medium.

2 Simmer for 40 minutes without skimming. Transfer the pork belly to another pot. Simmer in tare to cover for 20 minutes and drain; this will be your Iejiro Chashu.

3 Continue simmering the broth. Stir frequently with a wooden spatula to encourage emulsification.

4 After one hour, turn off the heat and transfer the back fat to a bowl. Break into small pieces using a whisk. You will have about 11 oz (330 g) of cooked back fat.

5 Pour the broth through a fine mesh strainer.

Pro Tips

- Stirring the broth as it cooks promotes emulsification, resulting in a rich, thick broth.
- Pig's feet are rich in gelatin and umami, perfect for making a flavorful soup in a short time.

Pro Tips

- Mix the ingredients thoroughly before heating to prevent burning.
- Reserve the minced garlic from the cooked tare to add to Iejiro Ramen or Dipping Noodles.
- Don't use high-quality "hon-mirin" in this recipe. A cheap "aji-mirin" is a better match for this fast-food-style sauce.

Iejiro Tare

It's not Iejiro without garlic! The goal of this tare is to go all out with bold, fast-food-like flavors.

Serves 4

2/3 cup (150 ml) dark soy sauce
3 tablespoons + 1 teaspoon mirin
1 tablespoon sugar
3 teaspoons umami seasoning, such as MSG
3 cloves garlic

Iejiro Mazesoba, page 64

Iejiro Dipping Noodles, page 65

Taiwan Mazesoba, page 76

1 Mince the garlic. Combine all the ingredients in a saucepan and mix well.

2 Bring to a boil over high heat. Remove from heat and pour through a fine mesh strainer. Reserve the garlic to use in Iejiro Ramen or Iejiro Dipping Noodles.

Pro Tips

- Increase the amount of vegetables, garlic, pork back fat and noodles to taste. More is more with Iejiro Ramen
- Fresh linguine or fettuccine is a close approximation of the thick, chewy noodles served at Ramen Jiro restaurants.

Iejiro Ramen

Perfectly recreate the Ramen Jiro flavor at home. This recipe is my definitive take on fast-food-style ramen.

Serves 1

7 oz (200 g) fresh linguine

For the soup:

1 cup plus 2 tablespoons (270 ml) Iejiro Broth (page 60)
3 tablespoons plus 1 teaspoon Iejiro Tare (page 62)
4 tablespoons Iejiro Pork Back Fat (page 60)

For the toppings:

2 cups (400 g) bean sprouts
2 cabbage leaves, roughly chopped
3 slices Iejiro Chashu, or more (page 60)
1 clove garlic, minced
Garlic reserved from making Iejiro Tare, to taste (page 62)
Iejiro Pork Back Fat, to taste (page 60)

1 Bring 2 pots of water to a boil, one for the noodles and one for the vegetables.
2 Warm the broth in a small saucepan. Place in a serving bowl with the tare and back fat.
3 Boil the linguine until al dente. In the other pot, boil the bean sprouts and cabbage for 10 seconds. Drain the noodles and vegetables.
4 Add the noodles to the bowl. Garnish with the toppings.

Pro Tips

- I recommend using finely ground rather than coarsely ground white pepper.
- Sear the sliced chashu just before serving to make it juicy.
- At the restaurant, we mix the sauce and noodles together before adding the toppings. You can also let diners mix everything themselves.

Iejiro Mazesoba

Mazesoba means "mixed noodles," and this version is seriously addictive. The addition of Baby Star ramen snack noodles enhances the junk food factor. Great with a beer!

Serves 1

1 hank fresh "tsukemen" ramen noodles, 4 to 5 oz (130 g) or 7 oz (200 g) fresh linguine

For the sauce:

1 tablespoon + 2 teaspoons Iejiro Tare (page 62)
4 tablespoons Iejiro Pork Back Fat (page 60)
White pepper to taste

For the toppings:

¼ cup (50 g) bean sprouts
2 leaves cabbage, roughly chopped
2 slices Iejiro Chashu (page 60)
1 tablespoon Baby Star brand ramen snack noodles
1½ tablespoons *gyofun* fish powder
1 tablespoon grated Parmesan
1 raw egg yolk from a very fresh or pasteurized egg, optional*

1 Put the tare and pork back fat in a serving bowl and sprinkle with white pepper.
2 Cook the ramen noodles or linguine in plenty of boiling water following package directions.
3 In a separate pot of boiling water, cook the bean sprouts and cabbage for about 10 seconds. Drain.
4 Drain the noodles well and add to the bowl. Thoroughly mix the noodles and sauce.
5 Warm a skillet over high heat and briefly sear the chashu.
6 Garnish the noodles with the toppings, adding the egg yolk last if using.

*Consuming raw eggs may increase your risk of food-borne illness.

Pro Tips

- Wash the noodles by rubbing them between the palms of your hands to remove the sticky starch. Wash in at least two changes of water, then drain well in a colander.

Iejiro Dipping Noodles

Tsukemen, or dipping noodles, get the Iejiro treatment in this recipe. The contrast between the chilled noodles and the hot dipping sauce is a key part of the appeal.

Serves 1

1 hank fresh "tsukemen" ramen noodles, 4 to 5 oz (130 g) or 7 oz (200 g) fresh fettuccine

For the sauce:

2 tablespoons + 2 teaspoons Iejiro Tare (page 62)
3 tablespoons + 1 teaspoon Iejiro Pork Back Fat (page 60)
2/3 cup (150 ml) Iejiro Broth (page 60)
Japanese ground chili pepper (*ichimi togarashi*) to taste
2 tablespoons thinly sliced green onion

For the toppings:

A handful of bean sprouts
2 leaves cabbage, roughly chopped
2 slices Iejiro Chashu (page 60)
1 clove garlic, minced
1 teaspoon garlic reserved from making Iejiro Tare (page 62)

1 Cook the noodles in plenty of boiling water for twice the length of time indicated on the package.
2 Combine the sauce ingredients in a small serving bowl. Microwave for 40 seconds.
3 Warm a small skillet over high heat and quickly sear the chashu.
4 Boil the bean sprouts and cabbage for 10 seconds. Drain.
5 Rinse the boiled noodles under cold running water until they are cool (see Pro Tips). Drain thoroughly and place in another serving bowl. Garnish with the toppings and serve with the sauce.

What Makes a Great Bowl of Ramen?

Ramen is made up of several key elements, including broth, tare, and fat—but which one is most important? The answer varies from restaurant to restaurant.

For me, the answer is different for each type of ramen. For example, the most important element of dried anchovy ramen is the broth. I might shock some people by saying this, but I think tare plays only a supporting role in this ramen. On the other hand, for some types of ramen, the tare is the most important part. It all depends on which element is the main source of umami. The role of fat is to tie together the broth and tare. I'm not impressed by ramen that relies on a thick layer of fat to make up for a poor broth and tare.

The only thing I can say is that there's no single right answer when it comes to ramen. This may sound strange, but when customers praise my ramen or say it's bad, it doesn't really affect me. That's because I believe each person has their own idea of what's delicious.

Once I went out for ramen at a restaurant called En in Hachioji, Tokyo. I loved it, but the person I was eating with was on the fence. That was a big turning point for me.

Just because you're impressed by something, that doesn't mean other people will be. In other words, like I said above, there's no single right answer when it comes to ramen. In my view, the best ramen is one that people either love or hate, not the one everyone thinks is decent. My goal has always been to make ramen no one has ever made before and give it a shot in the world.

Chapter 5

Homemade Regional Ramen

Sampling unique regional ramens is one of the joys of traveling in Japan. Everything from the noodles to the broth to the toppings can vary wildly from place to place! If you can't make it to Japan, recreating them at home is nearly as much fun.

Takeoka Ramen

This ramen from Takeoka, across the bay from Tokyo in Chiba Prefecture, is famous for its dark soup. The shoyu tare and raw onion topping make for an irresistible bowl.

Serves 1

1 package dried ramen noodles, 5 to 6 oz (150 g)
¾ cup (180 ml) water for cooking the noodles

For the soup:
⅔ cup (150 ml) water
4 tablespoons + 2 teaspoons All-Purpose Shoyu Tare (page 16)
2 teaspoons lard
A small pinch of umami seasoning, such as MSG

For the toppings:
⅓ cup (70 g) minced onion
5 slices chashu, homemade or store-bought
4 strips fermented bamboo shoot (*menma*)
1 snack-size sheet nori

1 Bring the water for the soup to a boil in one small pot, and the water for cooking the noodles to a boil in another small pot.
2 Cook the noodles following package directions. Drain, reserving the cooking water.
3 While the noodles cook, combine the tare, lard, and umami seasoning in a serving bowl. Add the noodle cooking water and the additional boiling water and mix well.
4 Add the noodles and garnish with the toppings.

Pro Tips

- Umenoya, the restaurant where Takeoka Ramen originated, uses Miyakoichi brand noodles. They are available online.

- This soup is unique in that it doesn't use broth. Instead, water from cooking the noodles is combined with extra hot water, tare and lard.

Tokushima Ramen

This ramen is soul food for residents of Tokushima, on the east coast of the island of Shikoku. The sweet-and-salty soup topped with a raw egg is very similar to sukiyaki.

Serves 1

1 hank fresh thick ramen noodles, 4 to 5 oz (130 g)

For the sliced pork belly (enough for two servings):

1 tablespoon + 1 teaspoon All-Purpose Shoyu Tare (page 16)
5 oz (150 g) thinly sliced pork belly

For the soup:

2 tablespoons + 2 teaspoons All-Purpose Shoyu Tare (page 16)
1 small clove garlic, grated
A pinch of umami seasoning, such as MSG
¼ teaspoon spicy bean paste (*doubanjiang*)
1¼ cups (300 ml) Chicken and Pork Paitan Broth (page 34)

For the toppings:

¼ cup (50 g) bean sprouts
3 tablespoons thinly sliced green onion
1 raw egg yolk from a very fresh or pasteurized egg*
5 strips fermented bamboo shoot (*menma*)

1 Cut the pork belly into pieces 2 inches (5 cm) wide.
2 Warm a skillet over medium heat. Add the pork belly and 1 tablespoon + 1 teaspoon tare. Stir-fry until cooked through.
3 Cook the noodles in plenty of boiling water following package directions. Add the bean sprouts 1 minute before the noodles are done, placing in a small strainer or basket to keep them separate if desired.
4 Put the remaining 2 tablespoons + 2 teaspoons of tare in a serving bowl with the garlic, umami seasoning and spicy bean paste. Warm the broth in a small saucepan and add to the bowl. Mix well.
5 Drain the noodles and sprouts and add to the bowl. Garnish with the toppings.

*Consuming raw eggs may increase your risk of food-borne illness.

Pro Tips

- I recommend using pork belly with plenty of fat.
- One or two teaspoons of sugar can be added at Step 2 for a sweeter flavor.

Onomichi Ramen

This fragrant, rich soup from Onomichi in Hiroshima Prefecture is very satisfying. The soup combines the umami of seafood, pork, and chicken, while the toppings include chunks of fatback as well as chashu.

Serves 1

1 hank fresh flat or thick ramen noodles, 4 to 5 oz (130 g)

For the soup:

2 tablespoons Favorite Shoyu Tare (dark version) (page 29)
1 heaping tablespoon Iejiro Pork Back Fat (page 60)
1½ tablespoons *gyofun* fish powder
A pinch of umami seasoning such as MSG, optional
1¼ cups (300 ml) Basic Mixed Broth (page 14)

For the toppings:

1 slice *naruto* fish cake
1 slice chashu, homemade or store-bought
5 strips fermented bamboo shoot (*menma*)
3 tablespoons sliced green onion
1 snack-size sheet nori

1 Cook the noodles in plenty of boiling water following package directions.
2 Combine the tare, pork back fat, fish powder and umami seasoning in a serving bowl.
3 Heat the broth in a small saucepan and add to the bowl.
4 Drain the noodles and add to the bowl. Garnish with the toppings.

Pro Tips

- For the best flavor, use a fish powder that blends several types of fish, such as bonito, mackerel and dried anchovies.

Nagasaki Chanpon Ramen

A specialty of Nagasaki, in western Japan, this ramen gets its delicious flavor from vegetables and seafood. The word *chanpon* originally meant "various things mixed together," and the secret to success here is the large number of ingredients.

Serves 1

1 hank thick ramen noodles, 4 to 5 oz (130 g)

4 cabbage leaves
1/2 small carrot
8 slices *kamaboko* fish cake
1 slice *satsumaage* fish cake
2 oz (60 g) thinly sliced pork belly
1 tablespoon + 1 teaspoon sesame oil
6 shrimp, peeled and deveined
1/2 cup (120 g) bean sprouts
2 tablespoons whole corn kernels
1 tablespoon boiled shelled edamame
1 1/4 teaspoons Chinese stock paste
White pepper to taste
2 tablespoons Shio Tare (page 28)
1 1/4 cups (300 ml) Chicken and Pork Paitan Broth (page 34)
1 teaspoon dark soy sauce

1 Roughly chop the cabbage. Slice the carrot and fish cake into thin strips. Cut the pork belly into ¾ inch (2 cm) wide strips.
2 Heat the sesame oil in a skillet over medium heat. Stir-fry the pork belly and shrimp.
3 When the shrimp turns pink, add the cabbage, carrot, bean sprouts, corn and edamame and stir-fry. When the bean sprouts have wilted, add the fish cake, stock paste and white pepper and stir-fry to combine.
4 Add the tare, broth and dark soy sauce and stir to combine.
5 Cook the noodles in plenty of boiling water following package directions. Drain and place in a serving bowl.
6 Pour the vegetable mixture over the noodles and serve.

Pro Tips

- The soup absorbs the flavors of the many ingredients added to it.
- For even more flavor, drizzle about a teaspoon of sesame oil over the ramen before serving.

Taiwan Mazesoba

Garlicky, spicy ground meat and miso stimulate the appetite in this mazesoba ("mixed noodle") recipe. Despite its name, Taiwan Mazesoba originated in Nagoya, Japan.

Serves 1

1 hank fresh "tsukemen" ramen noodles, 4 to 5 oz (130 g)
1 teaspoon Iejiro Tare (page 62) or dark soy sauce
4 tablespoons Iejiro Pork Back Fat (page 60)
White pepper to taste

For the spicy ground pork (enough for 4 servings):
1 tablespoon + 2 teaspoons sesame oil
2 cloves garlic, minced
12 oz (350 g) ground pork
½ cup (120 ml) dark soy sauce
1 red chili pepper, about ¼ oz (8 g), thinly sliced
2 scant teaspoons umami seasoning, such as MSG
3 tablespoons sugar

For the toppings:
1 green onion, sliced
¾ cup (30 g) chopped garlic chives
Shredded nori, to taste
1½ tablespoons *gyofun* fish powder
1 raw egg yolk from a very fresh or pasteurized egg
2 cloves garlic, minced

*Consuming raw eggs may increase your risk of food-borne illness.

1 To make the spicy ground pork, warm the sesame oil and minced garlic in a skillet over medium heat. When the oil is fragrant, add the ground pork and stir-fry until the color changes. Add the dark soy sauce, chili, umami seasoning and sugar. Stir-fry for 1 minute and remove from heat.
2 Combine the tare or dark soy sauce, pork back fat and white pepper in a serving bowl and whisk together.
3 Cook the noodles in plenty of boiling water following package directions. Drain and add to the bowl, tossing to combine. Top with ¼ of the Spicy Ground Pork and other toppings.

Pro Tips

- Add a scoop of cooked white rice to the bowl after you finish the noodles. For some, it's the best part of this meal!.

Kitakata Ramen

This light ramen is from Kitakata, in western Fukushima Prefecture, a city famous for its many ramen shops. Unlike some heavier broths, this is one you'll want to drink down.

Serves 1

1 hank fresh thick ramen noodles, 4 to 5 oz (130 g)

For the broth (enough for 3 to 4 servings):
6 cups (1½ l) water
1 lb (500 g) pork belly
1 leek or large green onion, green part only
1 oz (30 g) dried anchovies (*niboshi*)

For the chashu:
3 cups (800 ml) All-Purpose Shoyu Tare (page 16)

For the soup and toppings:
2 tablespoons Favorite Shoyu Tare (light version) (page 29)
1½ teaspoons lard
5 strips fermented bamboo shoot (*menma*)
3 tablespoons thinly sliced green onion

1 Combine the water, pork belly, leek or green onion and dried anchovies in a pot over high heat. When it comes to a boil, reduce the heat to low and simmer for 40 minutes.

2 Remove the pork belly. Pour the broth through a fine mesh strainer.

3 In a medium pot, simmer the boiled pork belly in the All-Purpose Shoyu Tare for 20 minutes to make the chashu.

4 Cook the noodles in plenty of boiling water following package instructions.

5 Combine the Favorite Shoyu Tare, lard and 1¼ cups (300 ml) of the broth from Step 2 in a serving bowl. Add the drained noodles. Garnish with as much sliced chashu from Step 3 as you want, along with the bamboo shoots and green onion.

Pro Tips

- Kitakata Ramen is best with freshly made, juicy chashu.

Tsubame Sanjo Ramen

Dried anchovies, pork back fat, and thick noodles pack a punch in this hearty ramen from northern Japan.

The soup stays piping hot thanks to the generous amount of fat. This ramen is made in the cities of Tsubame and Sanjo in Niigata Prefecture.

Serves 1

6 oz (180 g) fresh fettuccine

For the soup:
2 tablespoons All-Purpose Shoyu Tare (page 16)
4 tablespoons Iejiro Pork Back Fat (page 60)
1¼ cups (300 ml) Dried Anchovy Broth (page 30)

For the toppings:
2 slices Pork Belly Chashu (page 18)
4 tablespoons minced onion
5 strips fermented bamboo shoot (*menma*)
1 handful *aosa nori* seaweed

1 Cook the fettuccine in plenty of boiling water until al dente.
2 Put the tare and back fat in a serving bowl. Warm the broth in a small saucepan and add to the bowl.
3 Add the drained noodles to the bowl and garnish with the toppings.

Pro Tips

- Fresh fettuccine is a good substitute for the thick, chewy noodles traditionally served with this ramen.
- The onion and *aosa nori* balance the sweet, heavy pork back fat.

Kyoto Ramen

I occasionally get an irresistible urge to eat this ramen. Kyoto ramen is somewhere between the light ramen of Tokyo and the rich, thick ramen of Kyushu—a "light-rich" ramen.

Serves 1

1 hank fresh thick ramen noodles, 4 to 5 oz (130 g)

For the soup:
2 tablespoons + 2 teaspoons All-Purpose Shoyu Tare (page 16)
1 tablespoon Iejiro Pork Back Fat (page 60)
A pinch of umami seasoning, such as MSG
¼ teaspoon spicy bean paste (*doubanjiang*)
1¼ cups (300 ml) Chicken and Pork Paitan Broth (page 34)

For the toppings:
¼ cup (50 g) bean sprouts
2 slices Pork Belly Chashu (page 18)
6 strips fermented bamboo shoot (*menma*)
2 tablespoons thinly sliced green onion
Japanese ground chili pepper (*ichimi togarashi*), to taste

1 Combine the tare, fat, umami seasoning and spicy bean paste in a serving bowl. Warm the broth in a small saucepan, add to the bowl and mix well.
2 Cook the noodles in plenty of boiling water following package directions.
3 Blanch the bean sprouts in another small pot of boiling water. Drain.
4 Drain the noodles and add to the bowl. Garnish with the toppings.

Pro Tips

- In Kyoto, cooks use a local type of leek called *kujo negi* that is sweet and delicious.
- The small amount of *doubanjiang* and pork back fat make this a subtly spicy and sweet ramen.

Dandan Noodles

Spicy and packed with umami! These noodles get their spice and brilliant red color from la-yu, a fragrant Japanese chili oil.

Serves 1

1 hank fresh thin ramen noodles, 4 to 5 oz (130 g)

4 green onions, white part only
½ medium onion
2 teaspoons vegetable oil
½ cup (80 g) Spicy Pork (page 91)
2 tablespoons Favorite Shoyu Tare (page 29)
1 tablespoon la-yu chili oil
1¼ cups (300 ml) Super Simple Chicken Broth (page 32)

1 Cut the green onion in half lengthwise, then shred on the diagonal. Rinse under running water and pat dry with a paper towel. Cut the onion into wedges, then cut each wedge in half crosswise.
2 Warm the oil in a skillet over medium heat and stir-fry the onion chunks. When the onion softens, add the Spicy Pork and stir-fry to combine.
3 Put the tare and la-yu in a serving bowl. Warm the broth in a small saucepan and add to the bowl.
4 Cook the noodles in plenty of boiling water following package directions. Drain and add to the bowl. Add the pork and onion mixture and top with the shredded green onion.

Pro Tips

- The spiciness of the la-yu chili oil is a perfect counterpoint to the sweetness of the onion chunks.
- This Japanese version of dandan noodles is different from the original Szechuan dish, but very tasty!

How Ramen Rotas Got Its Start

People sometimes ask me what "Rotas," the name of my restaurant, means. Actually, there's no profound significance behind it. I always thought the name AFURI, a restaurant in Ebisu, Tokyo, sounded cool, and I wanted to use a three-syllable name for my own restaurant (in Japanese, Rotas is pronounced *ro-ta-su*). In addition, the lotus (*rotasu* in Japanese) is the national flower of Vietnam, where I went on my honeymoon, and it made a lasting impression on me. That's how I arrived at Ramen Rotas!

It's been 12 years since my wife and I got married; we had gone to the same high school, where she was a year ahead of me. When we first opened the restaurant, we worked together all day, every day, but when our first child was born, my wife left the restaurant. She still gives me valuable feedback when she eats the ramen I make, though.

When we first opened, we decided to focus on just two items on the main menu: dried anchovy ramen and pork ramen, both personal favorites. They're on opposite ends of the spectrum; the former uses all-natural ingredients while the latter includes processed ingredients like MSG. This was how I expressed my love for the full rainbow of ramen. It was my way of saying there's no single right answer when it comes to ramen.

I think my strategy of attracting customers by focusing on ramen I'm confident in has been successful. Gradually, I increased the number of items on the menu because I like to take on new challenges. I'm sure I'll keep adding more, just to keep things interesting. Currently, I'm exploring new possibilities through videos. My goal, as always, is to share fun experiences through ramen.

Chapter 6

Sides, Snacks and Staff Meal Secrets

Sometimes, ramen isn't quite enough. In this chapter, I've shared some of the other dishes I serve at the restaurant, both to customers and to my staff. Several make use of the leftovers from preparing broth or flavored fat. Humble ingredients like boiled ground chicken, dried anchovies and chicken skins are transformed into wonderful side dishes or snacks to enjoy with drinks!

Ramen Restaurant Fried Rice

Lard is the secret ingredient in this moist fried rice. It only takes about 5 minutes to cook, and is a great way to use up leftover rice.

Serves 1

1-inch piece (20 g) *naruto* fish cake
1 slice chashu (30 g), homemade or store-bought
1 tablespoon + 1 teaspoon lard
1 teaspoon sesame oil
2 eggs, beaten
1 cup (220 g) cooked short-grain white rice
½ teaspoon salt
A pinch of umami seasoning, such as MSG
1½ tablespoons minced onion
2 teaspoons All-Purpose Shoyu Tare (page 16)
2 tablespoons thinly sliced green onion

1 Chop the fish cake and chashu into ¼ inch (7 mm) cubes.
2 Heat the lard and sesame oil in a wok and tilt to coat the surface.
3 Add the beaten egg to the wok, and before the egg sets add the rice. Break the rice and egg apart with a ladle as you stir-fry.
4 Add the salt and umami seasoning and stir-fry for another minute or two. Add the onion, chashu and fish cake and continue stir-frying to heat through.
5 Drizzle the tare down the side of the wok. Add the green onion and stir-fry briefly to combine.

Pro Tips

- I recommend lard over vegetable oil for stir-frying.
- Using two eggs rather than one gives the egg a robust presence in the fried rice.
- MSG is a popular seasoning among home cooks in Japan. Mushroom-based umami seasonings are also available.
- Adding the green onion at the end makes a more aromatic fried rice.

Green Onion and Chashu with Rice

If you have some Pork Belly Chashu and All-Purpose Shoyu Tare on hand from making ramen, this is a perfect quick meal. Make sure not to slice the green onion too thinly, so some texture remains when it's cooked.

Serves 1

2 large green onions
4 slices (100 g) Pork Belly Chashu (page 18)
1 teaspoon vegetable oil
1 teaspoon Chinese stock paste
2 teaspoons All-Purpose Shoyu Tare (page 16)
½ cup (120 g) warm cooked short-grain white rice

1 Cut the green onions in half lengthwise, then slice on the diagonal ¼ inch (7mm) thick.
2 Sear the chashu lightly over a gas burner or in a hot skillet. Cut into strips ¼ inch (7 mm) wide.
3 Warm the oil in a skillet over medium heat. Add the green onion and stock paste and stir-fry over medium heat.
4 When the green onion is wilted, add the chashu strips and tare and stir-fry to combine.
5 Serve the stir-fry over the rice.

Pro Tips

- A rule of thumb when thickening a stir-fry with cornstarch is to dissolve it in twice as much water as starch before adding to the skillet.

Mapo Tomato Bowl

Just the right balance of spicy and sour. Mapo tofu is a classic Chinese dish, but it's surprisingly delicious made with tomatoes instead of tofu.

Serves 1

2 teaspoons sesame oil
1 large tomato, cut in big chunks
1 teaspoon cornstarch
2 teaspoons water
½ cup (120 g) warm cooked short-grain white rice
2 tablespoons thinly sliced green onion
Szechuan pepper, to taste

For the Spicy Pork (enough for 3 servings):
1 tablespoon plus 1 teaspoon vegetable oil
7 oz (200 g) ground pork
2 tablespoons plus 1 teaspoon spicy bean paste (*doubanjiang*)
1 teaspoon sweet bean paste (*tianmianjiang*)
1 teaspoon Korean spicy bean paste (*gochujang*)
1½ teaspoons umami seasoning, such as MSG
2 tablespoons mirin

1 To make the Spicy Pork, heat the vegetable oil in a skillet and stir-fry the pork. When the meat changes color, add the three bean pastes, umami seasoning and mirin and stir-fry until the liquid evaporates. Remove the pork from the skillet and reserve.

2 Heat the sesame oil in the same skillet and stir-fry the tomato.

3 When the tomato begins to soften, add a third of the Spicy Pork and stir-fry to combine.

4 Dissolve the cornstarch in the water and add to the skillet, stirring until thickened. Serve the meat and tomatoes over the warm rice. Top with the green onion and Szechuan pepper.

Staff Meal Curry

The sweet-and-sour flavor of this curry is addictive. To make it, you'll need to buy a box of instant Japanese curry roux—curry powder or sauce can't be substituted.

Serves 3 to 4

1 onion
1 clove garlic
8 oz (250 g) thinly sliced pork belly
1 tablespoon plus 1 teaspoon lard
1 teaspoon spicy bean paste (*doubanjiang*)
2½ cups (600 ml) Basic Mixed Broth (page 14), Super Simple Chicken Broth (page 32) or Chicken and Pork Paitan Broth (page 34)
⅔ cup (150 ml) vegetable juice
½ cup (100 ml) pineapple juice
2 teaspoons oyster sauce
Commercial Japanese curry roux, to taste
1 teaspoon la-yu chili oil
Warm cooked short-grain white rice

1 Cut the onion into wedges and mince the garlic. Cut the pork belly into strips 2 inches (5 cm) wide.
2 Melt the lard in a pot over medium heat and stir-fry the pork belly.
3 When the pork belly is almost cooked through, add the onion, garlic and spicy bean paste and stir-fry for a few minutes.
4 Add the broth, vegetable juice, pineapple juice, oyster sauce and half a box of curry roux.
5 When the liquid comes to a boil, turn off the heat and stir in more curry roux to taste.
6 Simmer over low heat until thickened. Drizzle with the la-yu and serve with the rice.

Pro Tips

- Broth gives the curry a full flavor without having to stew it for a long time.
- I recommend using the thick, rich Chicken and Pork Paitan Soup. If you don't have enough broth you can combine it with water or broth made from stock granules.
- The spicy bean paste, oyster sauce and vegetable juice all add umami.

Gyoza Dumplings

These juicy pan-fried dumplings are a classic ramen restaurant side dish. There's a bit of a learning curve to making them at home, but once you master the technique, it's very fast. Check out the gyoza video on my YouTube channel to see the method in action.

Makes 50

1 bunch garlic chives, 3½ oz (100 g)
½ small cabbage, 10 oz (300 g)
2 stalks celery, 2½ oz (70 g)
4 green onions, 3 oz (80 g)
1 egg
2 tablespoons cornstarch
50 gyoza skins
3 tablespoons sesame oil, divided
3 tablespoons + 1 teaspoon boiling water

For the meat mixture:
12 oz (350 g) ground pork
4 cloves garlic, minced
2-inch (5-cm) piece ginger, minced
⅓ teaspoon salt
½ teaspoon black pepper
1 tablespoon plus 1 teaspoon cooking sake
1 teaspoon fish sauce (*nam pla*)
1 tablespoon miso
1 tablespoon plus 1 teaspoon Chinese stock paste
¾ teaspoon sugar

1 Combine all the ingredients for the meat mixture in a bowl and mix well with your hands until the meat is sticky. Refrigerate for 30 minutes to 1 hour.
2 Cut the garlic chives into pieces ⅕ inch (5 mm) long. Finely chop the cabbage, celery and green onion in a food processor.
3 Combine the garlic chives and chopped vegetables with the meat mixture. Add the egg, cornstarch and 1 tablespoon of sesame oil and mix well. Place a spoonful of filling on each gyoza skin, fold over and pleat to seal.
4 Warm 1 tablespoon of sesame oil in a large skillet over medium heat. Carefully arrange the filled gyoza in the skillet, nestling them in a circular pattern, and brown the bottoms.
5 Add the hot water and immediately put on a lid to steam the gyoza.
6 When the skins turn translucent, add the remaining tablespoon of sesame oil and crisp the skins to finish. Serve with the dipping sauce of your choice.

Pro Tips

- The basic protein-to-vegetables ratio for gyoza is 1:1.
- The filling is easier to handle when cold, so refrigerate it if you have time.
- At Step 5, be sure to use boiling water so the temperature in the skillet does not fall.

Plated Wontons

Enjoy these dumplings with beer for lunch on a day off. The juicy filling and refreshing vinegar-soy sauce make them highly addictive.

Makes 25

4 oz (100 g) ground pork
1½ teaspoons All-Purpose Shoyu Tare (page 16)
2 tablespoons minced green onion
1 teaspoon minced or grated ginger
1 teaspoon cornstarch
A small pinch umami seasoning, such as MSG
A small pinch salt
25 wonton skins, store-bought
Thinly sliced green onion, to taste

For the sauce:
1 clove garlic, minced
3 tablespoons + 1 teaspoon All-Purpose Shoyu Tare (page 16)
1 teaspoon rice vinegar
1 teaspoon la-yu chili oil or sesame oil
Szechuan pepper to taste

1 Put the ground pork in a bowl and break up with your hands.
2 Add the 1½ teaspoons tare, green onion, ginger, cornstarch, umami seasoning and salt to the meat and mix well.
3 Place a small amount of filling in the middle of each wonton skin. Fold in half and press to seal.
4 To make the sauce, combine the ingredients in a small bowl.
5 Cook the wontons in plenty of boiling water for 2½ minutes.
6 Drain the wontons and arrange on a plate. Pour the sauce over them and top with the sliced green onion.

Pro Tips

- Komatsuna is a mild, quick-cooking Japanese green with a bit more heft than spinach. Baby bok choy or chard make good substitutes.

Stir-Fried Greens with Ground Chicken

This healthy and delicious stir-fry makes use of boiled ground chicken left over from making broth. Serve it over rice for a quick meal or snack on days when you are prepping the elements for ramen.

Serves 1 to 2

1 bunch komatsuna greens, 5 oz (150 g)
1 teaspoon Chinese stock paste
1 tablespoon All-Purpose Shoyu Tare (page 16)
1 tablespoon + 1 teaspoon sesame oil
1 clove garlic, minced
2/3 cup (150 g) boiled ground chicken from making Basic Mixed Broth (page 14) or Super Simple Chicken Broth (page 32)
1 teaspoon spicy bean paste (*doubanjiang*)
1 teaspoon oyster sauce
Coarsely ground black pepper to taste

1 Cut the komatsuna into pieces 2 inches (5 cm) wide, keeping the leaves and stems separate.
2 Combine the stock paste and tare in a small bowl and mix well.
3 Warm the sesame oil in a skillet and stir fry the garlic over low heat until fragrant.
4 Add the ground chicken, spicy bean paste and oyster sauce and stir-fry over medium heat to combine.
5 Add the komatsuna stems and stir-fry over high heat until they begin to soften.
6 Add the komatsuna leaves and the tare mixture and stir-fry just until the komatsuna wilts. Transfer to a serving dish and top with black pepper.

Fresh Spring Rolls with Chicken Chashu

A special-occasion dish that can be made in 20 minutes if you have Lazy Chicken Chashu on hand. *Nam pla* fish sauce and crunchy nuts elevate this recipe to restaurant level.

Makes 8 rolls

½ medium red onion
½ yellow bell pepper
2 cups (90 g) mizuna greens
1 mini cucumber or small Japanese cucumber
⅓ recipe (160 g) Lazy Chicken Chashu (page 37)
16 medium shrimp, peeled and deveined
5 tablespoons mixed nuts, finely chopped
8 rice paper wrappers
A few sprigs cilantro

For the sauce:
1 tablespoon *nam pla* fish sauce
⅛ lemon
La-yu chili oil to taste
1 tablespoon mixed nuts, chopped

1 Thinly slice the red onion. Cut the bell pepper and cucumber into thin strips. Cut the mizuna greens into 2-inch (5-cm) pieces. Cut the chicken into slices ⅓ inch (1 cm) thick.
2 Boil the shrimp until they turn pink. Drain.
3 Dip a wrapper in a bowl of warm water. Arrange an eighth of the vegetables, nuts, chicken and shrimp on the wrapper in that order. Roll up like a burrito. Repeat with the rest of the wrappers and filling.
4 To make the sauce, combine the *nam pla*, juice from the lemon, la-yu and nuts in a small serving dish.
5 Arrange the spring rolls on a plate and garnish with cilantro.

Pro Tips

- When filling the wrappers, place ingredients you want to be visible, such as the shrimp, on top.
- Spread out the vegetables evenly on the wrapper.
- Fold in both sides of the wrapper before rolling from the bottom up.
- Roll tightly to keep the filling in place.

Chicken Cracklings with Ponzu

This classic Japanese pub dish transforms leftovers from rendering chicken fat into a delicious snack. Mizuna greens and lemon provide a refreshing contrast to the fatty skins.

Serves 1 to 2

1 cup (80 g) chicken skin left over from making Aromatic Fat (page 17) or Chicken Fat (page 36)
A pinch of salt
Black pepper to taste
1 tablespoon cornstarch
1 tablespoon vegetable oil
⅔ cup (30 g) mizuna greens
1 tablespoon + 1 teaspoon ponzu sauce, store-bought
Thinly sliced green onion, to taste
Toasted white sesame seeds, to taste
⅛ lemon

1 Cut the chicken skin into bite-sized pieces. Place in a bowl with the salt, pepper and cornstarch and toss to coat.
2 Heat the vegetable oil in a skillet. Cook the chicken skins over low heat until very crispy.
3 Cut the mizuna greens into 2-inch (5-cm) pieces and arrange on a serving dish. Top with the chicken skins. Drizzle with the ponzu sauce and top with the green onion and sesame seeds. Serve with the lemon wedge.

Pro Tips

- The chicken skins burn easily, so watch the heat.
- The flavorful cracklings are also delicious served on their own for snacking, without the greens, ponzu, and toppings.

Crunchy Anchovy Chili Crisp

This spicy-and-savory condiment uses up the dried anchovies left over from making broth. Once you try it, you may be tempted to make ramen just so you can enjoy this dish!

Makes about 1 cup

1 tablespoon vegetable oil
3 tablespoons + 1 teaspoon sesame oil
5 tablespoons minced garlic
5 tablespoons minecd onion
1/2 cup (100 g) boiled dried anchovies from making Basic Mixed Broth (page 14) or Dried Anchovy Broth (page 30)
3 tablespoons shredded dried squid (*sakiika*), cut in small pieces, optional
3 tablespoons minced red bell pepper
5 tablespoons chopped mixed nuts
1 1/2 teaspoons Chinese stock paste
1 tablespoon Japanese spice mix (*shichimi togarashi*)
3/4 teaspoon sugar

1 Coat a skillet with the vegetable oil and sesame oil. Add the garlic and onion and cook over medium heat until the garlic is golden brown.

2 Remove the garlic and onion from the skillet with a skimmer or slotted spoon.

3 Add the anchovies, squid, red bell pepper, mixed nuts, stock paste, spice mix and sugar to the skillet and cook over low heat for about 5 minutes, stirring occasionally.

4 Add the cooked garlic and onion and stir to combine.

Pro Tips

- Be careful not to let the garlic and onion burn.
- This chili crisp is incredible with plain steamed rice. You can also use it as a condiment with fried rice, noodles, eggs, vegetables, or just about anything else!

Chinese Style Pickles

A tasty side dish to have on hand. Pickles have never tasted better, thanks to the oyster sauce!

Serves 4 to 5

1 celery stalk
1 small red bell pepper
1 small yellow bell pepper
1 mini cucumber or small Japanese cucumber
Szechuan pepper to taste

For the brine:
1 cup (250 ml) rice vinegar
2 cups (450 ml) water
6 tablespoons sugar
1 tablespoon salt
2 teaspoons oyster sauce
¹⁄₄ teaspoon sesame oil

1 Cut the celery, bell peppers and cucumber into sticks.
2 Combine the brine ingredients in a storage container and mix well.
3 Add the vegetables and refrigerate overnight. Sprinkle with Szechuan pepper when serving.

Pro Tips

- These pickles are best eaten 3 to 4 days after making them.
- They will keep in the refrigerator for about a week.
- At Ramen Rotas, we use them to top Chilled Ramen (page 56).

A Few Final Thoughts

Thanks so much for picking up this book and reading it to the end! I am very grateful to viewers of the Ramen Rotas channel on YouTube who sought the book out, as well as to those who found it by chance on the internet or in a bookshop.

Some time ago, a friend who has traveled around the world said something that stuck with me.

"Everyone smiles when they're eating."

All over the world, even though cultures and languages differ, he said this was the one commonality everywhere he went.

Is that true, I wonder?

I definitely have some regular customers at Ramen Rotas who look really happy as they eat their ramen. It's almost as if they're doing it on purpose. The way they look when they slurp their noodles and drink the soup shows that they cherish every moment of eating the ramen I make for them.

A while after my friend said that, I asked my wife, "When do you feel happy?"

Do you know what she said?

That's right. "When I'm eating something delicious."

I'm convinced that eating enriches life.

So by all means, cook delicious ramen and make the people around you happy!

Finally, I'd like to express my heartfelt thanks to my beloved family and the staff who always support me.

—Shigekazu Takanashi,
Owner, Ramen Rotas

ROTAS
ROTAS

"Books to Span the East and West"

Tuttle Publishing was founded in 1832 in the small New England town of Rutland, Vermont [USA]. Our core values remain as strong today as they were then—to publish best-in-class books which bring people together one page at a time. In 1948, we established a publishing outpost in Japan—and Tuttle is now a leader in publishing English-language books about the arts, languages and cultures of Asia. The world has become a much smaller place today and Asia's economic and cultural influence has grown. Yet the need for meaningful dialogue and information about this diverse region has never been greater. Over the past seven decades, Tuttle has published thousands of books on subjects ranging from martial arts and paper crafts to language learning and literature—and our talented authors, illustrators, designers and photographers have won many prestigious awards. We welcome you to explore the wealth of information available on Asia at **www.tuttlepublishing.com**.

Published by Tuttle Publishing, an imprint of Periplus Editions (HK) Ltd.

www.tuttlepublishing.com

Gokujyou no Ouchi Ramen

English Translation by Makiko Itoh

Library of Congress Cataloging-in-Publication Data in process

ISBN 978-4-8053-1962-8

29 28 27 26 25 10 9 8 7 6 5 4 3 2 1
Printed in China 2504CM

Distributed by
North America, Latin America & Europe
Tuttle Publishing
364 Innovation Drive
North Clarendon, VT 05759-9436 U.S.A.
Tel: 1 (802) 773-8930
Fax: 1 (802) 773-6993
info@tuttlepublishing.com
www.tuttlepublishing.com

Japan
Tuttle Publishing
Yaekari Building, 3rd Floor
5-4-12 Osaki
Shinagawa-ku
Tokyo 141 0032
Tel: (81) 3 5437-0171
Fax: (81) 3 5437-0755
sales@tuttle.co.jp
www.tuttle.co.jp

Asia Pacific
Berkeley Books Pte. Ltd.
3 Kallang Sector #04-01
Singapore 349278
Tel: (65) 6741 2178
Fax: (65) 6741 2179
inquiries@periplus.com.sg
www.tuttlepublishing.com